# Eat God's Food

Susan U. Neal RN, MBA, MHS
illustrated by Courtney Smith

Copyright Notice
*Eat God's Food*
First edition. Copyright © 2021 by Susan U. Neal. The information contained in this book is the intellectual property of Susan U. Neal and is governed by United States and International copyright laws. All rights reserved. No part of this publication, either text or image, may be used for any purpose other than personal use. Therefore, reproduction, modification, storage in a retrieval system, or retransmission, in any form or by any means, electronic, mechanical, or otherwise, for reasons other than personal use, except for brief quotations for reviews or articles and promotions, is strictly prohibited without prior written permission by the publisher.

Scripture quotations marked HCSB are taken from the Holman Christian Standard Bible®, Used by Permission HCSB ©1999,2000,2002,2003,2009 Holman Bible Publishers. Holman Christian Standard Bible®, Holman CSB®, and HCSB® are federally registered trademarks of Holman Bible Publishers.

Scriptures marked NLT are taken from the HOLY BIBLE, NEW LIVING TRANSLATION (NLT): Scriptures taken from the HOLY BIBLE, NEW LIVING TRANSLATION, Copyright© 1996, 2004, 2007 by Tyndale House Foundation. Used by permission of Tyndale House Publishers, Inc., Carol Stream, Illinois 60188. All rights reserved. Used by permission.

Cover and Interior Design: Courtney Smith, Derinda Babcock
Editor(s): Derinda Babcock, Deb Haggerty

PUBLISHED BY: Elk Lake Publishing, Inc., 35 Dogwood Drive, Plymouth, MA 02360, 2021

---

Library Cataloging Data
Names: Neal, Susan U. (Susan U. Neal)
*Eat God's Food* / Susan U. Neal
58 p. 21.6cm × 21.6cm (8.5in × 8.5 in.)
ISBN-13: 978-1-64949-289-0 (paperback) | 978-1-64949-290-6 (trade hardcover) | 978-1-64949-291-3 (trade paperback) | 978-1-64949-292-0 (e-book)
Key Words: Kids educational workbook; books for preschoolers; activity book for Kindergarten; children's activity book; Christian children's books; healthy eating, good nutrition

# Table of Contents

Why Did God Plant a Garden?........................................... 3
Why Did God Give You Fruit?............................................ 7
    Fun Fruit Activity ................................................. 8
    *Let's Cook!* Frozen Berries ..................................... 10
Why Did God Give You Vegetables?................................... 12
    Vegetable Variety Activity ...................................... 14
    *Let's Cook!* Baked Yellow Squash ............................. 19
Why Did God Give You Grains?......................................... 21
    Amazing Grains Activity ........................................ 22
    *Let's Cook!* Banana Quinoa Oatmeal ......................... 23
Why Did God Give You Nuts?........................................... 25
    Nutty Matching .................................................. 26
    *Let's Cook!* Almond Butter .................................... 27
Why Did God Give You Seeds to Eat?................................. 29
    Seed Matching................................................... 30
    *Let's Cook!* Trail Mix ........................................... 31
Why Did God Give You Meat and Seafood?.......................... 33
    Seek and Find Foods High in Protein........................... 34
    *Let's Cook!* Baked Chicken..................................... 35
Why Are Fruits and Vegetables Seasonal?............................ 37

Seasonal Activity . . . . . . . . . . . . . . . . . . . . . . . . . . . . . 38
*Let's Cook!* Organic Popcorn . . . . . . . . . . . . . . . . . . . . 39
Why Did God Give You a Variety of Food? . . . . . . . . . . . . . . 41
Seek and Find Fruit . . . . . . . . . . . . . . . . . . . . . . . . . . 42
*Let's Cook!* Snack Bags . . . . . . . . . . . . . . . . . . . . . . . . 43
Why Did God Give You Water to Drink? . . . . . . . . . . . . . . . 45
Why Should You Avoid Junk Food? . . . . . . . . . . . . . . . . . . 47
Food Label Clues . . . . . . . . . . . . . . . . . . . . . . . . . . . . 49
*Let's Cook!* Granola . . . . . . . . . . . . . . . . . . . . . . . . . . 50
Why Should You Eat God's Foods? . . . . . . . . . . . . . . . . . . . 51
About the Author . . . . . . . . . . . . . . . . . . . . . . . . . . . . . . . 52
About the Illustrator . . . . . . . . . . . . . . . . . . . . . . . . . . . . . 53

# Introduction

Do you want to grow to be the strongest, smartest, healthiest kid you can be? Then eat the foods God created for you. This book will help you learn which foods are good for you and which ones are bad. It's full of fun facts and activities like matching games, seek-and-find puzzles, and recipes for delicious foods you can make with the help of an adult. By reading this book, you will even learn how to read food labels. Turn the page and find out why God planted a garden. You can start eating God's amazing foods today.

# Why Did God Plant a Garden?

Did you know God was a gardener? He planted the very first garden in Eden. In that special place, God created many different kinds of plants.

A lot of those plants produced food for Adam and Eve to eat. God's plants grew fruits, vegetables, grains, nuts, and seeds in different shapes, sizes, flavors, and colors.

Take a peek into God's garden. The red berries on the blueberry bushes are not quite ripe yet. If you ate one, the taste would be tart. Buzzing bees are gathering nectar from each flower on the squash vine. Pole beans are climbing corn stalks. The yellow silk tip on each ear of corn is starting to turn brown, which means they are ripe.

Everywhere Adam and Eve turned in that garden, they could find tasty, healthy foods. God provided everything they needed to eat. He has also made all of the foods from the Garden of Eden available to you today. Every good thing you need to eat to grow strong and healthy, God created.

Genesis 2:8–9 says, "The Lord God planted a garden in Eden. The Lord God caused to grow every tree good for food (HCSB)."

# Why Did God Give You Fruit?

Fruits are sweet and delicious. They are God's candy. They satisfy your sweet tooth. Just think of biting into a juicy strawberry, a tangy green apple, or a crunchy pomegranate.

Fruits also give your body fiber and vitamins you need to be healthy. Fiber helps your body move food smoothly through your digestive system, which makes going to the bathroom easier. Vitamins strengthen your bones and muscles and help all your organs to work well like God created them to.

# Fun Fruit Activity

Count the different types of fruit listed below you have eaten. How many new fruits do you have left to try? What colors are they?

**FRUIT**  **COLOR**

Apple  _____
Apricot  _____
Banana  _____
Blueberry  _____
Blackberry  _____
Cantaloupe  _____
Cherry  _____
Cranberry  _____
Currant  _____
Date  _____
Fig  _____
Grape  _____
Grapefruit  _____
Guava  _____
Honeydew melon  _____
Kiwi  _____

| FRUIT | COLOR |
|---|---|
| Kumquat | _____ |
| Lemon | _____ |
| Lime | _____ |
| Mango | _____ |
| Nectarine | _____ |
| Orange | _____ |
| Papaya | _____ |
| Peach | _____ |
| Pear | _____ |
| Persimmon | _____ |
| Pineapple | _____ |
| Plum | _____ |
| Pomegranate | _____ |
| Raspberry | _____ |
| Starfruit | _____ |
| Strawberry | _____ |
| Tangerine | _____ |
| Watermelon | _____ |

#_____ fruits you have eaten

#_____ fruits you need to try

# Let's Cook!

## Frozen Berries

Either pick or purchase any kind of berries you want. Strawberries need to be organic. Rinse with water and drain in a colander. Place berries on an ungreased cookie sheet. Make sure the berries do not touch each other.

Place the cookie sheet in the freezer for several hours until frozen. Place frozen berries in mason jars and put in the freezer.

Since each berry is frozen separately, you can take as many or as few out of the jar as you need when making a fruit smoothie. Crunch on frozen blueberries as a snack.

# Why Did God Give You Vegetables?

God created over one hundred different vegetables. He knew some of you would be picky eaters. Your body needs different nutrients to grow and work well.

**NUTRIENTS** is a big word for the things in foods that give you strength and energy. Vegetables have lots of nutrients. For example, spinach is loaded with vitamin A to help your eyes see better. Broccoli is full of B vitamins that help your body grow.

God gave us a variety of vegetables to choose from to make sure you get the right amount of vitamins you need. One of your jobs is to take care of your body. Eating different kinds and colors of vegetables helps you do a good job.

# Vegetable Variety Activity

Count the kinds of vegetables you have eaten. What vegetables have you never heard of? How many new vegetables do you need to try? What do they look like? Try drawing some.

Acorn squash

Artichoke

Asparagus

Avocado

Beet

Bell pepper

Black bean

Black-eyed pea

Bok choy

Broad bean

Broccoli

Brussels sprouts

Butternut squash

**DRAW A VEGETABLE IN EACH BOX**

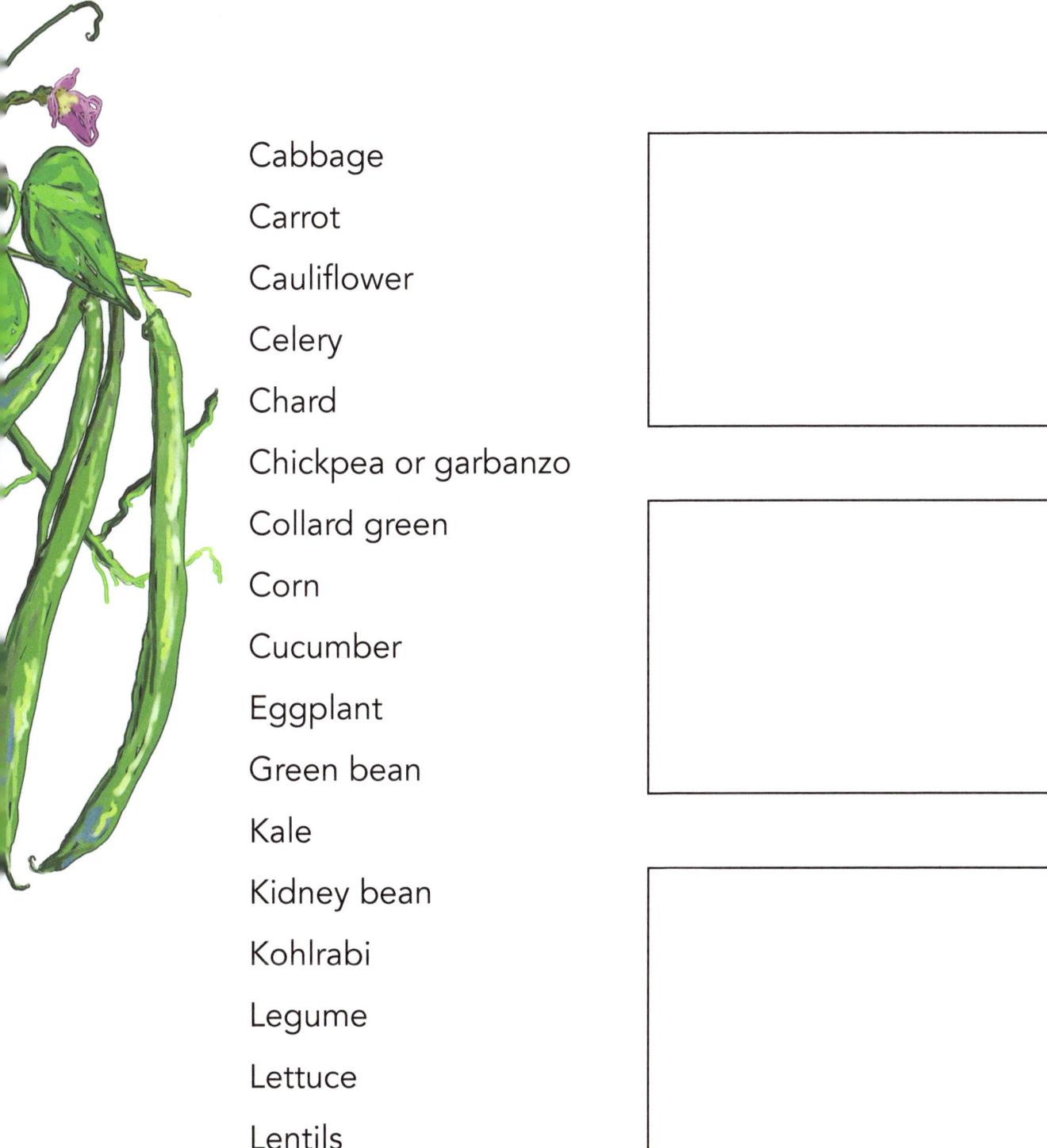

Cabbage

Carrot

Cauliflower

Celery

Chard

Chickpea or garbanzo

Collard green

Corn

Cucumber

Eggplant

Green bean

Kale

Kidney bean

Kohlrabi

Legume

Lettuce

Lentils

Lima bean or butter bean

Mustard greens

Navy bean

Okra

Onion family

Parsnip

Pattypan squash

Peas

Peppers

Pinto bean

Potato

Pumpkin

Radish

Rhubarb

Rutabaga

Snap peas

Soybean

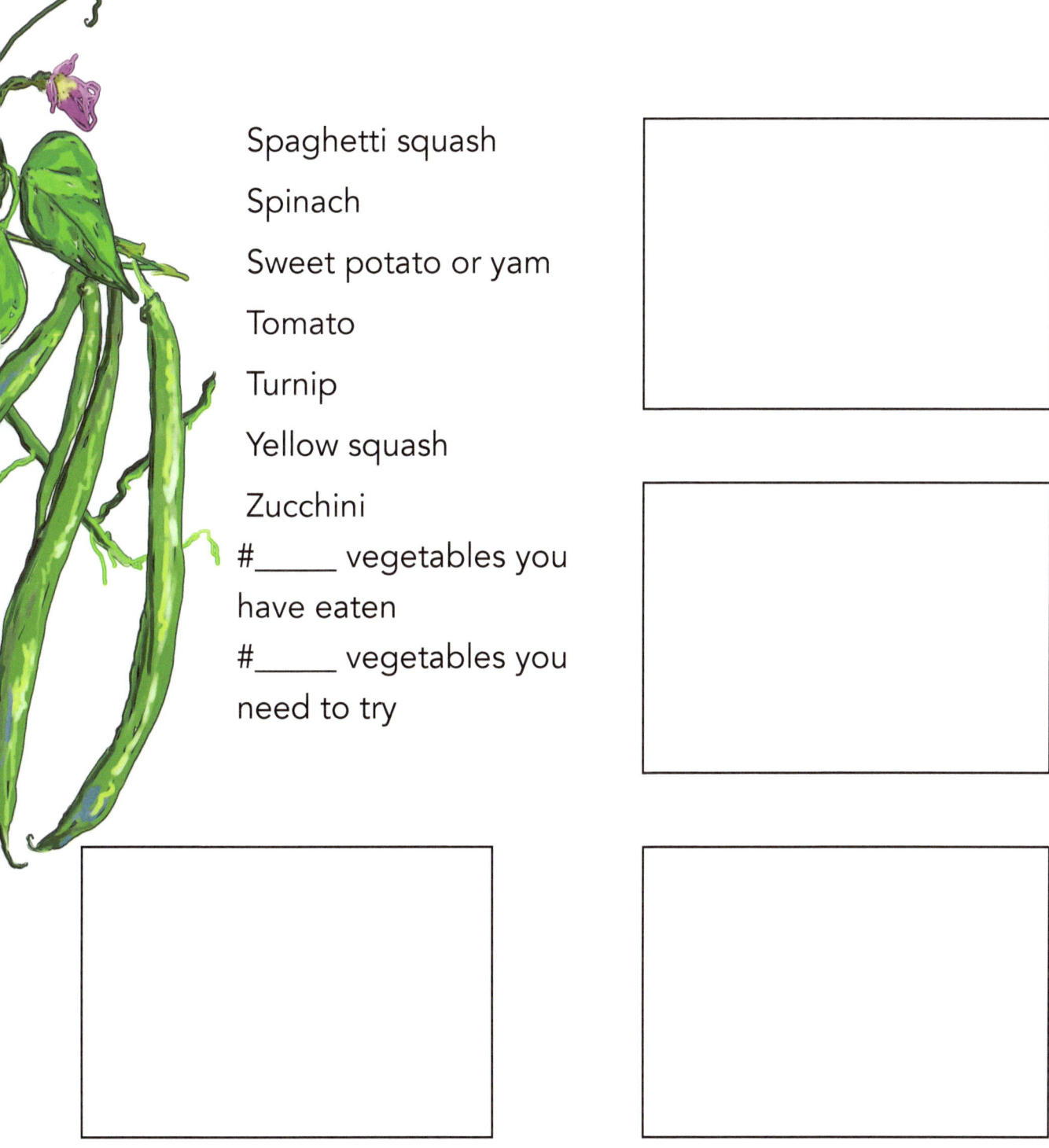

Spaghetti squash

Spinach

Sweet potato or yam

Tomato

Turnip

Yellow squash

Zucchini

#_____ vegetables you have eaten

#_____ vegetables you need to try

# Let's Cook!

## Baked Yellow Squash

4 yellow squash
2 tablespoons organic cornmeal
Olive oil cooking spray

Preheat oven to 400°F. Thinly slice yellow squash. Place 2 tablespoons of organic cornmeal in a plastic bag. Add the sliced squash and shake. Spray a baking pan with olive oil. Put squash slices on the pan so they are not touching. Spray the squash with the oil. Bake for 20 minutes or until lightly browned and crisp. Sprinkle with salt.

# Why Did God Give You Grains?

Just like a car needs gas to run, your body needs fuel or energy. Grains give the body energy through carbohydrates. God offers many grains to choose from. Runners usually eat a meal with lots of carbohydrates the evening before a race. This extra fuel helps them run fast for a longer period. That's how powerful grains are.

> Have you eaten all of these grains?
> rice, wheat, oats, wild rice, amaranth, barley, buckwheat, millet, quinoa, and rye

# Amazing Grains Activity

Match the correct grain with the picture. Which amazing grains have you never heard of?

1. ___ Rice          a.

2. ___ Wheat         b.

3. ___ Oats          c.

4. ___ Wild rice     d.

5. ___ Amaranth      e.

6. ___ Barley        f.

7. ___ Buckwheat     g.

8. ___ Millet        h.

9. ___ Quinoa        i.

10. ___ Rye          j.

ANSWERS: 1f, 2i, 3b, 4h, 5a, 6j, 7c, 8g, 9e, 10d

# Let's Cook!

## Banana Quinoa Oatmeal

1 cup of quinoa cooked in 2 cups of water (about 4 cups cooked)
2 smashed slightly green bananas (lower in sugar if green)
3/4 cup chopped walnuts
1 teaspoon cinnamon
1 teaspoon vanilla
honey or stevia to taste
3/4 cup almond or coconut milk

After the quinoa has cooked for 20 minutes, combine the rest of the ingredients in the pan and warm on the stove top.

# Why Did God Give You Nuts?

Nuts are packed with protein. Protein helps your body grow. Again, God gave us many types to choose from. Do you like nuts? What type of nut trees grow in your area? Could you go to a nut orchard and buy some?

> **Have you eaten all of these nuts?**
> almond, brazil, cashew, chestnut, hazelnut, macadamia, pecan, pistachio, pine nut, and walnut

> Peanuts are not a nut, but a type of vegetable called a legume (i.e., pea or bean). They grow in the ground and don't come from a tree. Nuts come from trees. Have you ever seen a walnut or pecan tree?

# Nutty Matching

Match the nut with the correct picture. Which ones have you eaten? Which ones do you like?

1. ___ Almond        a.

2. ___ Brazil        b.

3. ___ Cashew        c.

4. ___ Chestnut      d.

5. ___ Hazelnut      e.

6. ___ Macadamia     f.

7. ___ Pecan         g.

8. ___ Pistachio     h.

9. ___ Pine nut      i.

10. ___ Walnut       j.

ANSWERS: 1.b, 2.f, 3.h, 4.i, 5.g, 6.a, 7.j, 8.e, 9.c, 10.d

# Let's Cook!

## Almond Butter

Bake almonds for 15 minutes at 325°F on an ungreased cookie sheet. Let almonds cool. Place them in a food processor. Blend on high for about 7–10 minutes. Stop and stir the mixture about every minute.

(If you like crunchy nut butter, take a few tablespoons of nuts out of the food processor after blending it for about 30 seconds. Set aside five tablespoons for a two-cup mixture. Finish blending the nuts in the processor. Then add the reserved chopped nuts to the butter.) Store in the refrigerator.

# Why Did God Give You Seeds to Eat?

Seeds are full of trace minerals. Your body needs these in small amounts. Minerals keep your heart, brain, and muscles working well. God knows what you need. He provides these nutrients in many different foods.

> What seed will you try next?
> chia, flax, hemp, poppy, pumpkin, sesame,
> or sunflower seeds

# Seed Matching

Match the seed with the correct picture. Have you tried all of them?

1. \_\_\_ Chia
2. \_\_\_ Flax
3. \_\_\_ Hemp
4. \_\_\_ Poppy
5. \_\_\_ Pumpkin
6. \_\_\_ Sesame
7. \_\_\_ Sunflower seeds

a.
b.
c.
d.
e.
f.
g.

ANSWERS: 1d, 2a, 3g, 4f, 5b, 6c, 7e

# Let's Cook!

## Trail Mix

2 cups almonds
2 cups walnuts
2 cups pecans
1 cup sunflower seeds
1/2 cup sesame seeds
3/4 cup raisins
3/4 cup craisins

Mix all ingredients together and store in the refrigerator.

# Why Did God Give You Meat and Seafood?

God told Noah, "All the animals of the earth, all the birds of the sky, and all the fish. I have given them to you for food, just as I have given you grain and vegetables" (Genesis 9:2–3 NLT). Meat is full of protein which helps you grow and heals your cuts and scrapes. Eating protein through meat or fish nourishes and strengthens your body. Most of what you eat, however, should be what God originally gave humans in the Garden of Eden—fruits, vegetables, grains, nuts, and seeds.

# Seek and Find Foods High in Protein

Can you find the foods that are high in protein like meat, nuts, and beans?

# Let's Cook!

## Baked Chicken

Chicken thighs or breasts
Salt
Pepper

Preheat oven to 400°F. Place chicken pieces on a greased baking pan. Salt and pepper each piece. Cook for 30 minutes. Take out of the oven and stick a cooking thermometer into the thickest part of the chicken. When the temperature is 165°F, the meat is done.

# Why Are Fruits and Vegetables Seasonal?

Fruits and vegetables are seasonal, which means farmers harvest different crops each season of the year (spring, summer, fall, winter). God supplies a delicious combination of fruit and vegetables each season. That way, you do not get tired of eating the same type of food. Your body may need the nutrients in the plant that is ripe during that season. For example, oranges are ripe in the winter when your body requires more vitamin C to prevent a cold. God thought of everything!

> **Seasonal Fruits and Vegetables**
> Strawberries are ripe in early spring.
> Okra and peas grow best in the summer.
> Pumpkins are full grown in the fall.
> Citrus fruit is picked in the winter.

# Seasonal Activity

Do you know what season each fruit or vegetable becomes ripe? Match the fruit with the season. Use SP for Spring, SU for Summer, F for fall, and W for Winter.

1. ___ Apples
2. ___ Blueberries
3. ___ Broccoli
4. ___ Lemon
5. ___ Lettuce
6. ___ Okra
7. ___ Watermelon

Spring
Summer
Fall
Winter

ANSWERS: 1. F, 2. SU, 3. SP, 4. W, 5. SP, 6. SU, 7. SU

# Let's Cook!

## Organic Popcorn

2 tablespoons coconut oil
1/4 cup organic popcorn kernels (1 serving)

Cook oil and popcorn on high in a pan with a lid on the stove top. Constantly shake pan while cooking.

Toppings: 1/2–1 tablespoon butter, 1 tablespoon olive oil or coconut oil, kelp, dulse (seaweed), sea salt

# Why Did God Give You a Variety of Food?

As you grow, you should become responsible for caring for your body. You do this by eating different foods from each of God's food groups. Sometimes, you get into the habit of eating the same food. Eating a variety of colorful foods is healthier.

Find out what fruits, vegetables, grains, nuts, and seeds your body loves. Have fun choosing different colors and tastes.

God knew what he was doing when he created nutrient-rich foods to make you the smartest, fastest, healthiest kid you can be. He loaded these foods with vitamins and minerals to make you grow to your greatest potential. God did not give us food in bags or boxes. Instead, he gave fresh food right from the plant or tree. That is what is healthiest. Choose fresh fruit or nuts next time you eat a snack.

# Seek and Find Fruit

Can you find all the fruits hidden on this page? What is your favorite fruit? Find the red apple, green apple, blackberry, strawberry, banana, orange, two blueberries, lemon, two cherries, and grapes.

# Let's Cook!

## Snack Bags

Create snacks to carry with you by placing nuts in a resealable bag. Put trail mix in another bag. Seeds in a third bag. Or mix them all up into one bag. Take these snacks with you when going to play sports or to an event.

# Why Did God Give You Water to Drink?

The human body is 75 percent water. People cannot survive for more than a few days without this liquid. Water flushes out bad stuff from your body and prevents dehydration. Dehydration is a big word which means you lose more fluid than you take in and you body doesn't work right.

You should drink the fluid God gave—water. Some people think drinking tea, juice, soda, or other drinks will satisfy their bodies' need for fluid, but they don't. Some of those drinks actually take water out of the body. Always drink lots of water.

Put lemon, lime, or berries in your water for flavor.

# Why Should You Avoid Junk Food?

Junk food does not help your body grow. If you mostly eat junk food instead of God's foods, you could harm your body. Obesity (very overweight) can be caused by eating too much junk food.

Companies that make some foods take out the nutrients from the wheat plant to create white flour. Products made with white flour last a long time in the pantry before they spoil. Food companies also add salt, sugar, and dyes to make their foods look and taste delicious. But they are bad for you. Foods made this way are called processed foods or junk foods. The more of these you eat, the unhealthier you become.

Junk food fills you up so you don't want to eat healthy food. You should avoid foods made with white flour and added sugar. Junk food tricks the taste buds so you think you like the taste of processed treats better than healthy foods. Eating junk food once or twice a week is okay, but these foods do not give your body the nutrients to grow properly. Instead of growing taller with more muscle, you may grow wider with more fat.

Once you stop eating junk food, something very interesting happens. Within a couple of weeks, your taste buds return to normal, and God's foods begin to taste good again. Take a few bites each time one is served. Natural foods don't have added salt or sugar. Instead, they are full of the vitamins and minerals you need.

> Avoid eating foods made with white flour such as cake, cupcakes, pie, crackers, bread, biscuits, rolls, muffins, pasta, pizza crust, pretzels, and macaroni.

> Avoid eating processed and sugary foods such as potato chips, white rice, cereals, soda, jellies/jams, sweetened yogurt, candy, and marshmallows.

# Food Label Clues

Check the following food labels for unhealthy items added to foods. How many unhealthy ingredients did you find?

> **Unhealthy ingredients:**
> sugar, corn syrup, dextrose, preservatives, artificial flavors, colors, or sweeteners, caffeine, white flour, hydrogenated oil

## CANDY

**Nutrition Facts**
Serving Size 13 ounces (38g)
Servings Per Container about 3.5
**Amount per Serving**
**Calories** 170     Calories from Fat 60
                                   % Daily Value**
**Total Fat** 6g                                9%
   Saturated Fat 6g                    18%
   Trans Fat 0g
**Cholesterol** 0mg                          0%
**Sodium** 100mg                              4%
**Total Carbohydrate** 28g              9%
   Dietery Fiber 1g                            0%
   Sugars 20g
**Protein** 1g

Vitamin A   0%   *   Vitamin C   0%
Calcium      4%   *   Iron              0%

Ingredients: Corn Syrup, Sugar, Vegetable Oil (Cocoa Butter, Palm, Shea, Sunflower and/or Safflower Oil): Nonfat Milk; Dextrose, Chocolate, Contains 2% Or Less of Brown Sugar, Whey (Milk, Mono And Diglycerides; Sodium Bicarbonate, Milk Fat, Salt, Resinous Glaze, Soy Lecithin, Tapioca Dextrin, Vanillin, Artificial Flavor.

* Percent Daily Values are based on a 2,000 calorie diet.

## SODA

**Nutrition Facts**
Serving Size 12 fluid ounces (355 ml)
Servings Per Container about 1
**Amount per Serving**
**Calories** 170     Calories from Fat 0
                                   % Daily Value**
**Total Fat** 0g                                9%
**Sodium** 60mg                               4%
**Total Carbohydrate** 46g              9%
   Sugars 46g
**Protein** 10g

Not a significant source of other nutrients.

Ingredients: Carbonated Water, High Fructose Corn Syrup, Concentrated Orange Juice, Citric Acid, Natural Flavor, Sodium Benzoate (Preserves Freshness), Caffeine, Sodium Citrate, Erythorbic Acid (Preserves Freshness), Gum Aragic, Calcium Disodium EDTA (To Protect Flavor), Brominated Vegetable Oil, Yellow 5

* Percent Daily Values are based on a 2,000 calorie diet.

# Let's Cook!

## Granola

8 cups organic oats
1 cup almonds
1 cup pecans
1 cup walnuts
1/2 cup sunflower seeds
1/3 cup sesame seeds
1/3 cup pumpkin seeds
3/4 cup coconut or olive oil
1/2–2/3 cup of honey

Combine all ingredients. Pour into two large, greased baking pans. Bake at 325°F for 15 minutes; take out and stir. Bake for another 15 minutes, stir and add the following ingredients: 1–2 cups of dried fruit—berries, dates, apricots, raisins, or craisins.

Cook for 5–8 more minutes. Store granola in two quart-sized mason jars. Put one on the kitchen counter and the other in the refrigerator. Makes two quarts.

# Why Should You Eat God's Foods?

God knew what he was doing when he created many different nutrient-rich foods for you to eat. They provide what your body needs. Plus, they are delicious. Take care of yourself through eating natural foods like fruits, vegetables, grains, nuts, and seeds as close to harvest as possible.

Every time you sit down to eat, decide whether God created the food, like a baked potato, or a food company created the food, like potato chips. When you eat foods God created, you grow to be the strongest and healthiest you can be.

What is one change you can make to improve your eating habits?

_____

_____

# About the Author

**SUSAN U. NEAL** RN, MBA, MHS, lives her life with a passion for helping others improve their health. She is a Certified Health and Wellness Coach with the American Association of Christian Counselors. Her mission is to improve the health of the body of Christ. She is the author of seven healthy living books including her newest publication *Solving the Gluten Puzzle*. Her award-winning best-seller is *7 Steps to Get Off Sugar and Carbohydrates*. The sequel *Christian Study Guide for 7 Steps to Get Off Sugar and Carbohydrates* helps many overcome a dysfunctional relationship with food. You can find Susan on SusanUNeal.com.

# About the Illustrator

**COURTNEY SMITH** grew up in southwestern Colorado and attended college at Regis University where she met and married a handsome rocket scientist. Together, they have welcomed five children and live in Franktown, Colorado. Courtney raises Great Pyrenees puppies, teaches CPR, travels internationally with USA Olympic wrestling hopefuls as an athletic trainer, and cheers on her children. In her free time, she loves to draw and sketch, creating images to enhance incredible stories.